CREATIVE COLOURING
FOR GROWN-UPS

JAPANESE
PATTERNS

First published in Great Britain in 2015 by
Michael O'Mara Books Limited
9 Lion Yard
Tremadoc Road
London SW4 7NQ

A CIP catalogue record for this book is available from the British Library.

Papers used by Michael O'Mara Books Limited are natural, recyclable products
made from wood grown in sustainable forests. The manufacturing processes
conform to the environmental regulations of the country of origin.

ISBN: 978-1-78243-408-5

3 4 5 6 7 8 9 10

www.mombooks.com

Cover design by Ana Bjezancevic
Cover illustration by Hannah Davies
Designed by Claire Cater

Illustrations by Angela Porter, Angelea Van Dam, Hannah Davies, Julia Buckley,
Rosalind Monks, Sally Moret, Shutterstock and Textile Candy.

Printed and bound in Spain

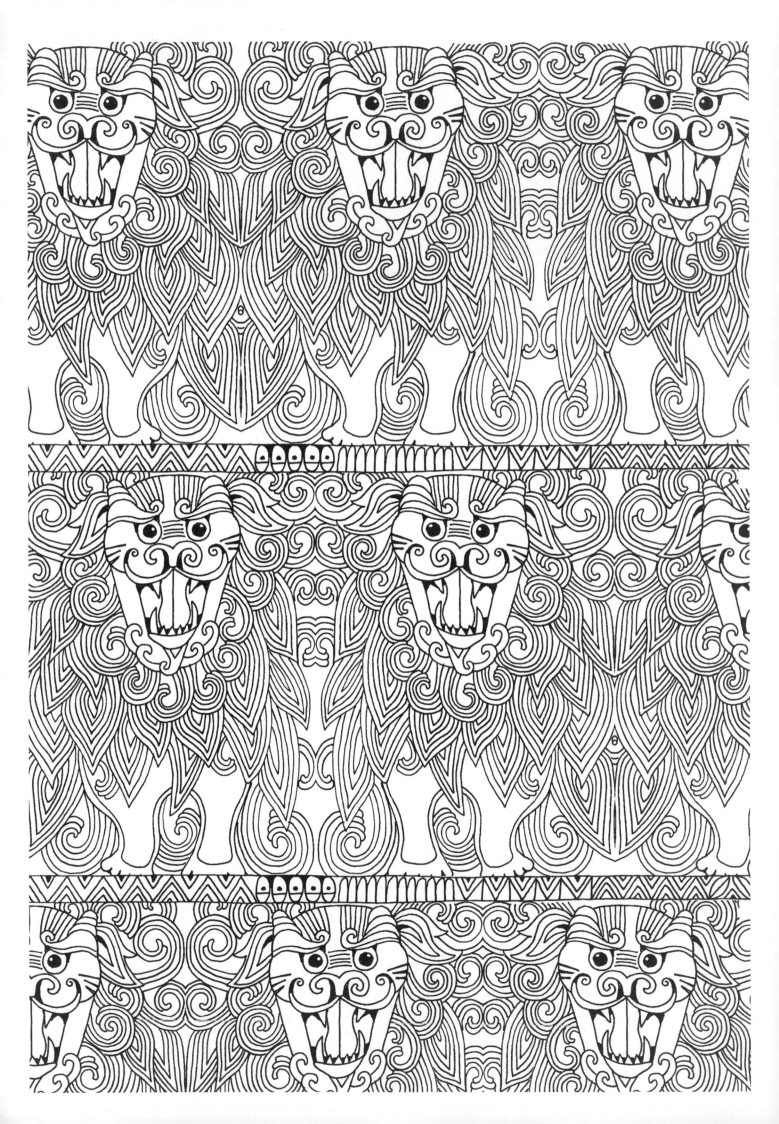

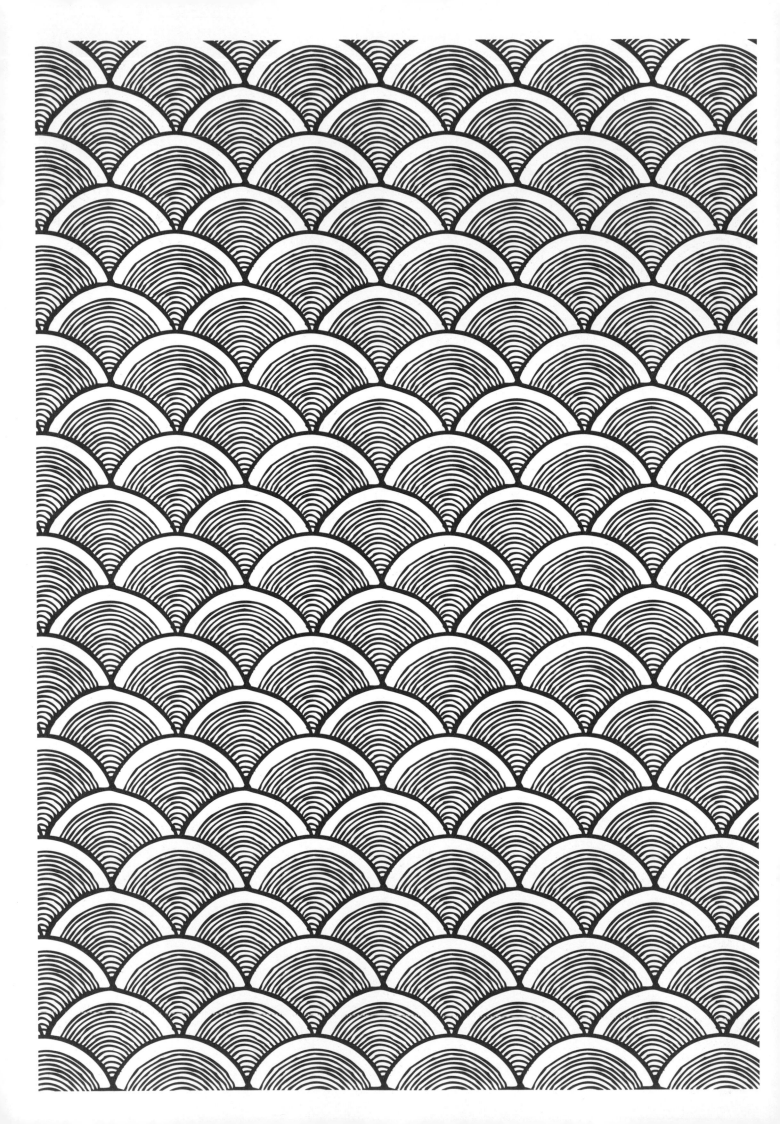

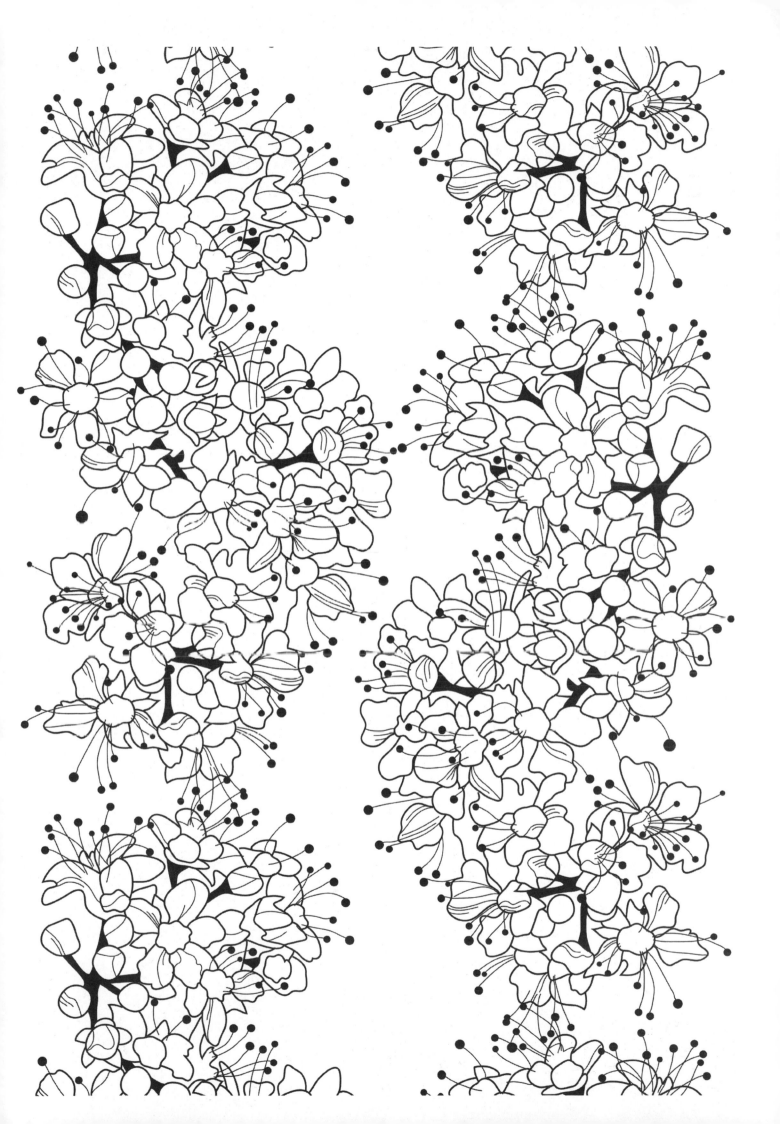

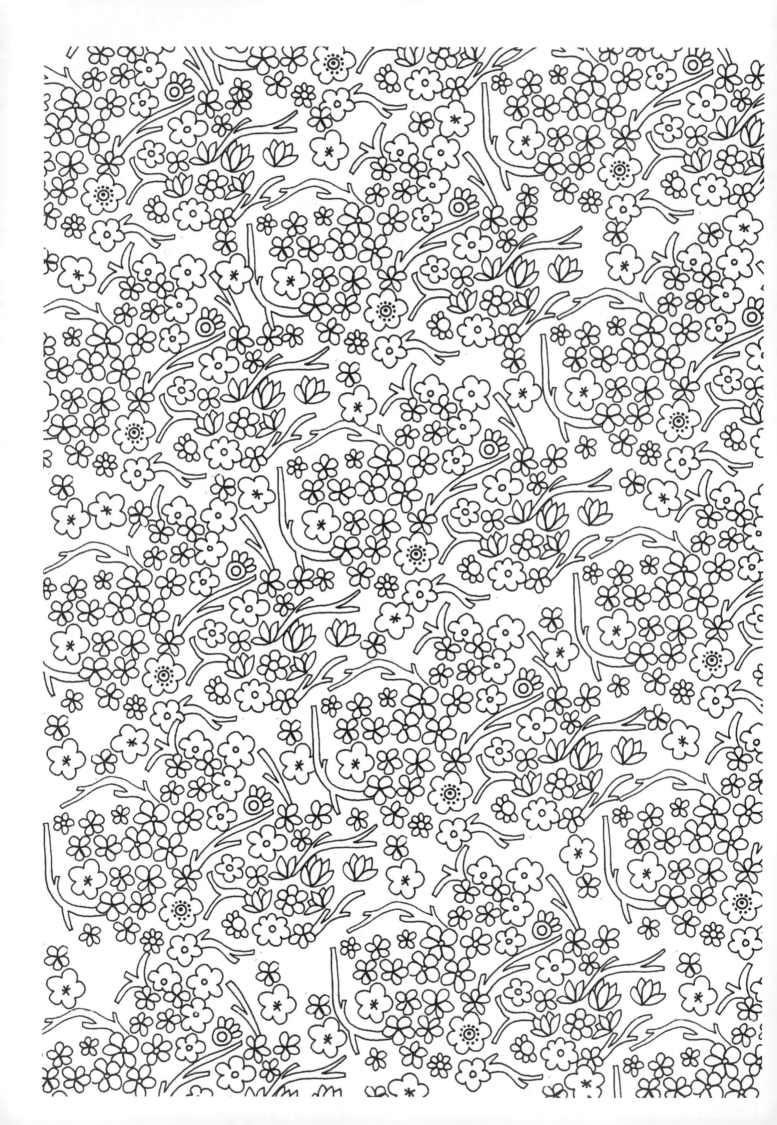

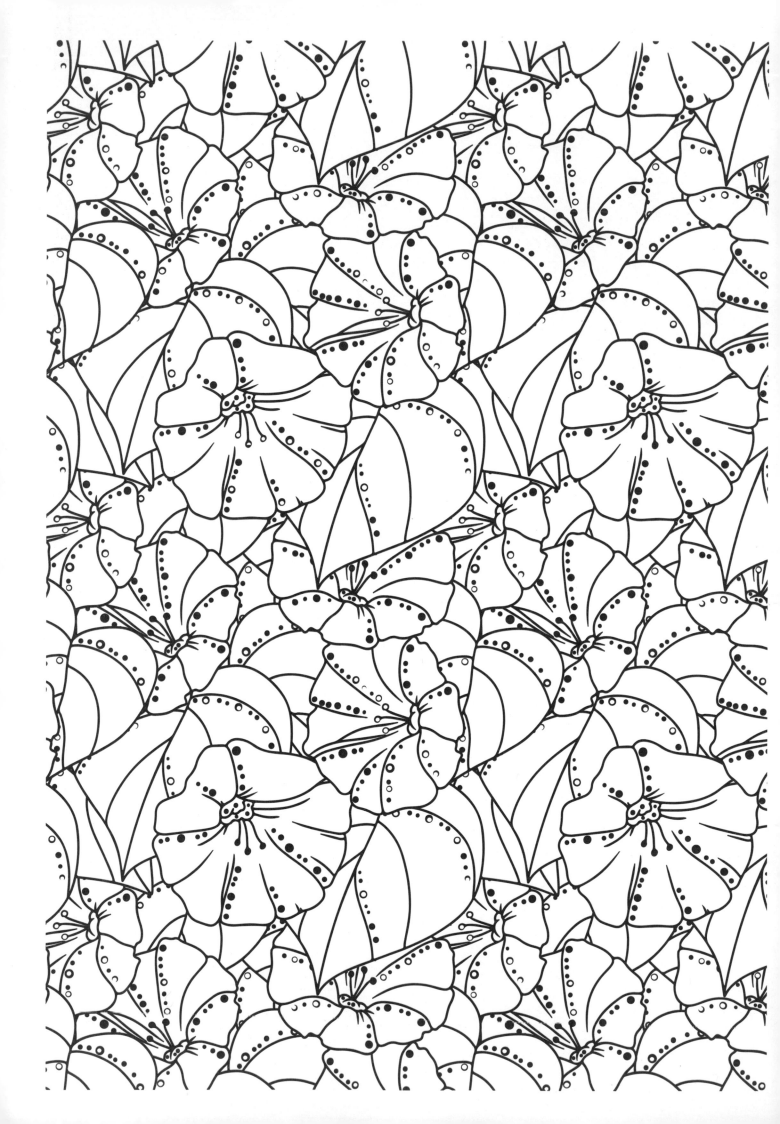

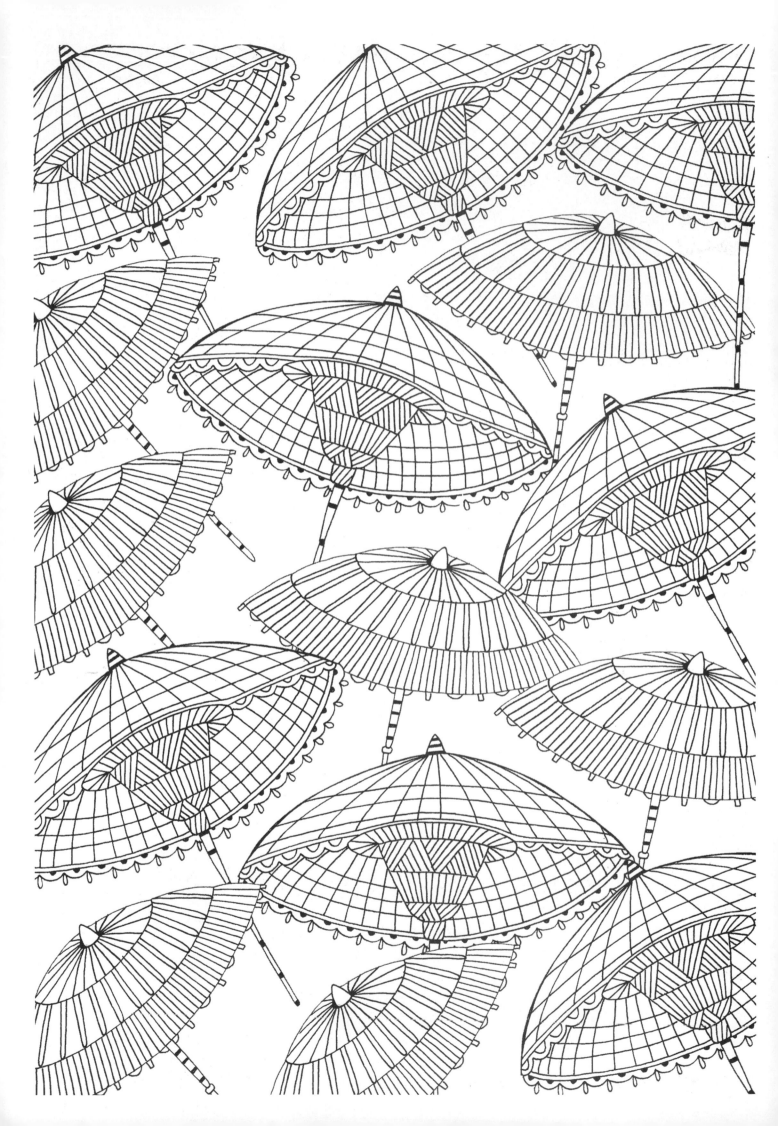

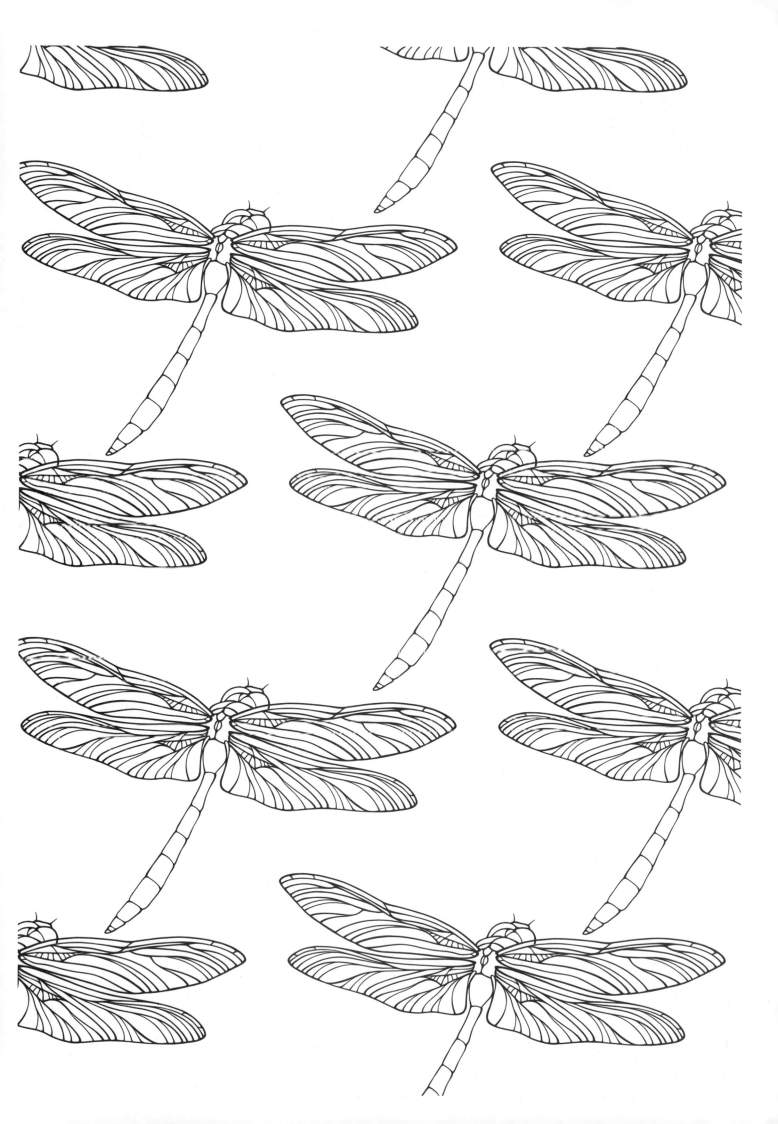

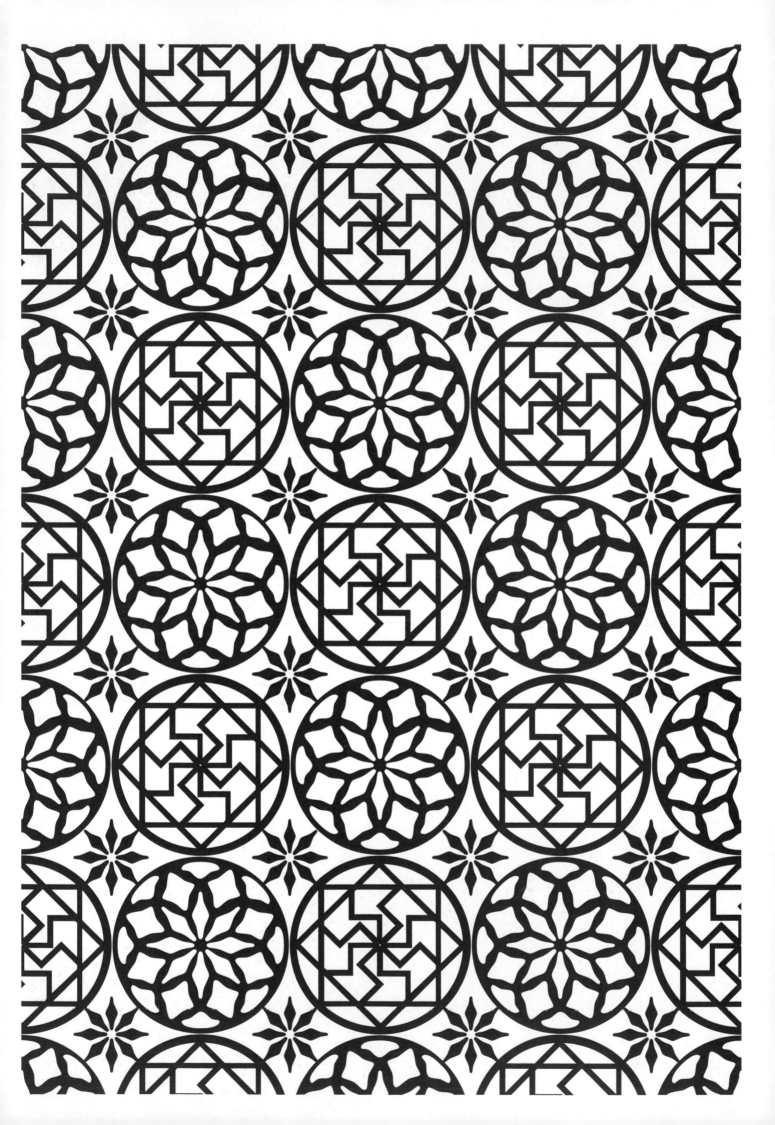

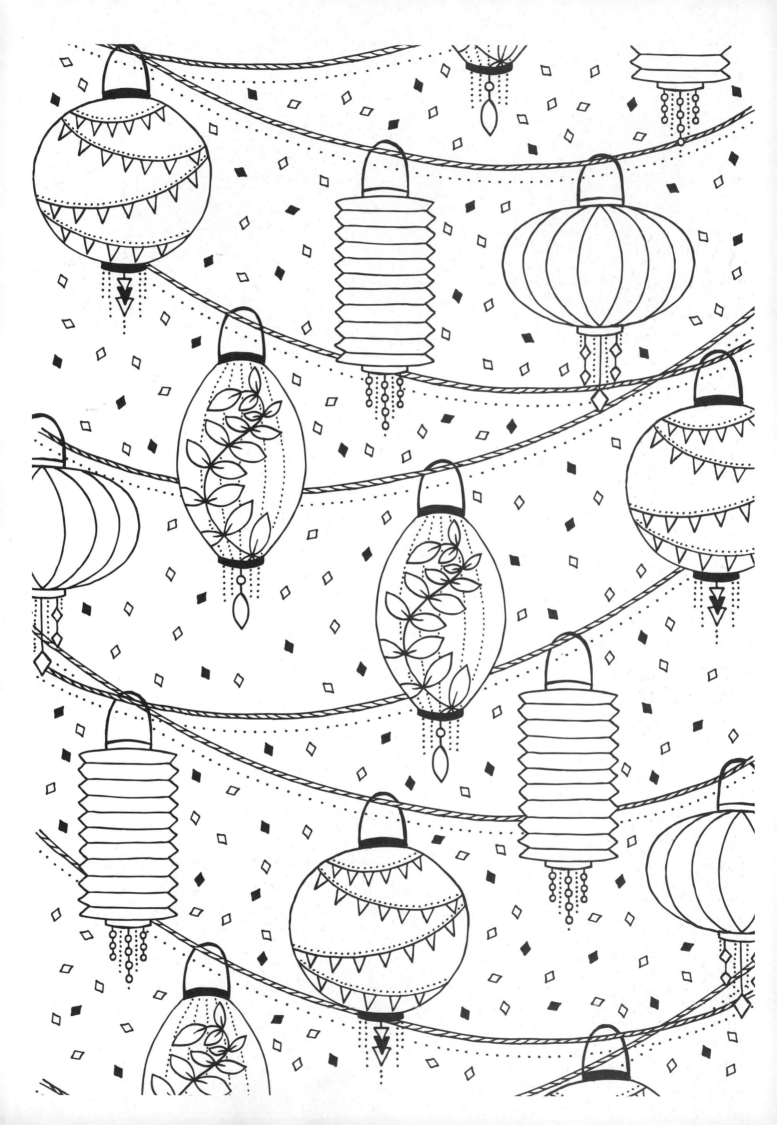